This book has been
typeset in Wallyfont

Printed in China

All rights reserved

British Library Cataloguing
in Publication Data:
a catalogue record for this
book is available from the
British Library.

ISBN 978-1-4063-1323-9

www.walkerbooks.co.uk

First published 1997 by
Walker Books Ltd
87 Vauxhall Walk
London SE11 5HJ

This edition published 2008

10 12 14 15 13 11

THIS WHERE'S WALLY? BOOK BELONGS TO:

_____

_____

HEY, WALLY FANS! FIVE INTREPID TRAVELLERS
ARE LOST IN EVERY SCENE! CAN YOU FIND THEM?

ODLAW   WIZARD   WENDA   WOOF   WALLY
         WHITEBEARD

AND IN EVERY SCENE, THE TRAVELLERS
HAVE EACH LOST SOMETHING PRECIOUS!
CAN YOU FIND THEM TOO?

WALLY'S KEY   WOOF'S BONE   WENDA'S CAMERA

WIZARD WHITEBEARD'S SCROLL   ODLAW'S BINOCULARS

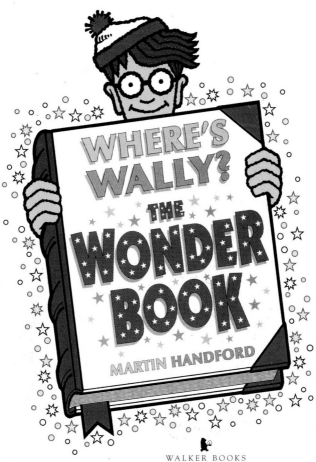

WHERE'S WALLY?
THE WONDER BOOK

MARTIN HANDFORD

WALKER BOOKS
AND SUBSIDIARIES
LONDON · BOSTON · SYDNEY · AUCKLAND

MUSIC

ONCE UPON A PAGE...

HEY, WALLY FANS! LOOK AT ALL THESE BRILLIANT BOOKS! LOOK AT ALL THE CHARACTERS WHO HAVE STEPPED OUT FROM THEIR PAGES! WOW! WHAT A MAGIC SCENE! THESE BOOKS HAVE REALLY COME ALIVE! FANTASTIC – THAT BOOK OVER THERE IS ABOUT MY TRAVELS! AND WOOF, WENDA, WIZARD WHITEBEARD AND ODLAW ALL HAVE SPECIAL BOOKS OF THEIR OWN. NOW YOU CAN JOIN US TOO, IF YOU CAN FIND US, AND WE'LL TRAVEL TOGETHER THROUGH ALL THE OTHER WONDERFUL SCENES IN THIS WONDER BOOK. ONE SCENE IS MY SPECIAL FAVOURITE – YOU'LL NEVER GUESS WHAT MAKES IT SO GREAT. THE BOOKMARK MARKS IT, SO WHEN WE GET THERE, YOU WILL KNOW. NOW GET SEARCHING, WALLY FOLLOWERS, AND OFF WE GO! AND BE PREPARED FOR LOTS OF SURPRISES ALONG THE WAY!

Wally

THE SEARCH IS ON! FIND THESE FIVE INTREPID TRAVELLERS IN EVERY SCENE IN THE WONDER BOOK!

- FIND WALLY ... WHO TRAVELS EVERYWHERE!
- FIND WOOF ... WHO WAGS HIS TAIL! (WHICH IS ALL YOU CAN SEE!)
- FIND WENDA ... WHO TAKES THE PICTURES!
- FIND WIZARD WHITEBEARD ... WHO CASTS THE SPELLS!
- FIND ODLAW ... WHOSE GOOD DEEDS ARE FEW INDEED!

THE SEARCH CONTINUES! NEXT FIND THESE IMPORTANT THINGS THE TRAVELLERS HAVE LOST!

- FIND WALLY'S LOST KEY!
- FIND WOOF'S LOST BONE!
- FIND WENDA'S LOST CAMERA!
- FIND WIZARD WHITEBEARD'S MAGIC SCROLL!
- FIND ODLAW'S LOST BINOCULARS!

THE GREAT BOOK OF ODLAW'S GOOD DEEDS

THE BOOK OF NURSERY RHYMES

CLASSIC STORIES FROM LITERATURE

WI... WHITE... BO... M...

THE MIGHTY FRUIT FIGHT

WOW! AMAZING! HAVE YOU EVER IN YOUR LIVES SEEN A PLACE SO FULL OF FRUIT? HOW SWEET IT IS TO SAIL LEMON BOATS DOWN ORANGE JUICE RIVERS! BUT WATCH OUT, WALLY FANS! THE APPLES HAVE TURNED SOUR AND THEY'RE ATTACKING ALL THE OTHER FRUIT. WHOOSH! SQUIRT! SPLOOOOOSH! THERE'S A FRUIT JAM IN THE RIVER, SCUFFLES ON THE BANANA BRIDGES AND SUGAR BEING POURED ALL OVER THE STRAWBERRIES! PHEW! WHAT A MIGHTY FRUIT FIGHT!

THE GAME OF GAMES

FOUR HUGE TEAMS ARE PLAYING THIS GREAT GAME OF GAMES. THE REFEREES ARE TRYING TO SEE THAT NO ONE BREAKS THE RULES. BETWEEN THE STARTING-LINE AT THE TOP AND THE FINISHING-LINE AT THE BOTTOM, THERE ARE LOTS OF PUZZLES, BOOBY-TRAPS AND TESTS. THE GREEN TEAMS NEARLY WON, AND THE ORANGE TEAMS HARDLY

STARTED! CAN YOU SPOT THE ONLY ORANGE TEAM PLAYER WHO HAS FINISHED? AND THE ONLY GREEN TEAM PLAYER WHO HAS NOT YET BEGUN?

5+4=9

2+2=7

TOYS! TOYS! TOYS!

WOW! ALL THE TEENY-TINY TOY CREATURES ARE COMING OUT OF THE TOYBOX TO EXPLORE THE PLAYROOM! THE BOOKS ARE TOO HUGE TO READ BUT THE GREEN ONE IS PERFECT AS A FOOTBALL PITCH! SWOOSH! AND THE BOOK-MARK MAKES A BRILLIANT SLIDE! CAN YOU SEE A TEDDY TAKING OFF IN A PAPER PLANE? AND A DINOSAUR CHASING A CAVEMAN? WHAT HIGH JINKS AND HIGH-WIRE ACTS ARE HAPPENING HERE! SO DO YOU THINK THAT THE TOYS ALWAYS HAVE GREAT TIMES LIKE THESE WHEN NO ONE IS ABOUT?

BRIGHT LIGHTS AND NIGHT FRIGHTS

HEY! WHAT BLAZING BEAMS OF LIGHT, WHAT A DAZZLING DISPLAY! GLITTER, TWINKLE, SPARKLE, FLASH – LOOK HOW BRIGHTLY THESE LIGHTHOUSES LIGHT UP THE NIGHT! BUT OH NO, THE MONSTERS WANT TO PUT THE LIGHTS OUT! THEY'RE ATTACKING FROM ALL SIDES. THE SAILORS ARE SQUIRTING PINK GUNGE AT THEM BUT THE MONSTERS SPURT GREEN GUNGE RIGHT BACK! BUT WAIT! THREE OF THE MONSTERS ARE FIRING DIFFERENT COLOURED GUNGE! SPLASH, SPLAT, SPLURGE! CAN YOU SEE THEM, WALLY-WATCHERS?

THE CAKE FACTORY

AT THE OOZING SUGAR ICING AND THE SHINY RED CHERRIES ON THE ROOF UP THERE! THAT ROOM IS WHERE THE FACTORY CONTROLLERS WORK, BUT HAVE THEY LOST CONTROL?

MMMM! FEAST YOUR EYES, WALLY-WATCHERS! SNIFF THE DELICIOUS SMELLS OF BAKING CAKES! DROOL AT THE TASTY TOPPINGS! CAN YOU SEE A CAKE LIKE A TEAPOT, A CAKE LIKE A HOUSE, A CAKE SO TALL A WORKER ON THE FLOOR ABOVE IS LICKING IT? CAKES, CAKES, EVERYWHERE! HOW SCRUMPTIOUS! HOW YUM-YUM-YUMPTIOUS! LOOK

THE BATTLE OF THE BANDS

THING! THEY ARE ALL DRESSED AS ANIMALS! SEE THE ELEPHANTS, THE BEARS, THE CROCS AND THE DUCKS! AND JUST LIKE THEIR MUSIC THEY ARE WILD AND WACKY!

BOOM, BOOM, RAT-A-TAT-TAT! HAVE YOU EVER HEARD SUCH A BEATING OF DRUMS! ROOT-A-TOOT TAN-TARA! OR SUCH AN EAR-SPLITTING BLAST OF TRUMPETS! A HOSTILE ARMY OF BANDSMEN IS MASSING BENEATH THE RAMPARTS OF THE GRAND CASTLE OF MUSIC. SOME ARE BEING PUSHED ALONG IN BANDSTANDS! OTHERS ARE CLIMBING MUSIC-NOTE LADDERS! BUT WHAT A STRANGE

THE ODLAW SWAMP

THE BRAVE ARMY OF MANY HATS IS TRYING TO GET THROUGH THIS FEARFUL SWAMP. HUNDREDS OF ODLAWS AND BLACK AND YELLOW SWAMP CREATURES ARE CAUSING TROUBLE IN THE UNDERGROWTH. THE REAL ODLAW IS THE ONE CLOSEST TO HIS LOST PAIR OF BINOCULARS. CAN YOU FIND HIM, X-RAY-EYED ONES? HOW MANY DIFFERENT KINDS OF HATS CAN YOU SEE ON THE SOLDIERS' HEADS? SQUELCH! SQUELCH! I'M GLAD I'M NOT IN THEIR SHOES! ESPECIALLY AS THEIR FEET ARE IN THE MURKY MUD!

CLOWN TOWN

Clap your feet, Wally Jokers! Stamp your hands! You'll go oogly-boogly-woogly-eyed with wonder! Here are hundreds of clowns playing pranks and making mischief! Look at their colourful costumes – with their fluffy pompoms galore! And their bright and shiny noses! Toot, toot! Can you see a car with its tongue sticking out?

Ting-a-ling! And a bike with square wheels! Tee, hee! Ha, ha! What happiness it is to be in Clown Town! Splash! Splat! Except for all those squirty flowers and custard pies!

THE FANTASTIC FLOWER GARDEN

WOW! WHAT A BRIGHT AND DAZZLING GARDEN SPECTACLE! ALL THE FLOWERS ARE IN FULL BLOOM, AND HUNDREDS OF BUSY GARDENERS ARE WATERING AND TENDING THEM. THE PETAL COSTUMES THEY ARE WEARING MAKE THEM LOOK LIKE FLOWERS THEMSELVES! VEGETABLES ARE GROWING IN THE GARDEN TOO. HOW MANY DIFFERENT KINDS

CAN YOU SEE? SNIFF THE AIR, WALLY FOLLOWERS! SMELL THE FANTASTIC SCENTS! WHAT A TREAT FOR YOUR NOSES AS WELL AS YOUR EYES!

THE CORRIDORS OF TIME

TICK-TOCK, TICK-TOCK! THE HANDS OF ALL THE CLOCKS EXCEPT ONE SAY A QUARTER TO TWELVE. WHAT A DING-DONG THERE WILL BE WHEN THEY STRIKE! CAN YOU FIND THE ONLY CLOCK THAT TELLS A DIFFERENT TIME? IN THIS SCENE ARE THIRTY-SEVEN DOORS. ABOVE EACH DOOR APPEARS THE SHAPE OF THE KEY THAT WILL UNLOCK IT. CAN YOU FIND THE KEYS IN THE CROWD, BRAINY ONES, AND MATCH THEM TO THE SHAPES? OH NO! ONE DOOR HAS NO SHAPE ABOVE IT! EVEN SO YOU MUST FIND ITS KEY!

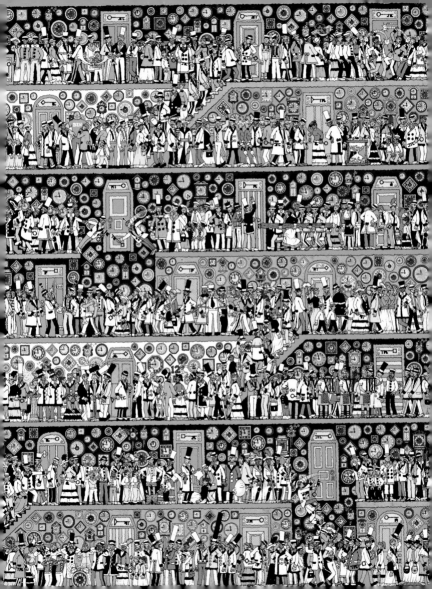

THE LAND OF WOOFS

HEY! LOOK AT ALL THESE DOGS THAT ARE DRESSED LIKE WOOF! BOW WOW WOW! IN THIS LAND, A DOG'S LIFE IS THE HIGH LIFE! THERE'S A LUXURY WOOF HOTEL WITH A BONE-SHAPED SWIMMING POOL, AND AT THE WOOF RACE TRACK LOTS OF WOOFS ARE CHASING ATTENDANTS DRESSED AS CATS, SAUSAGES AND POSTMEN! THE BOOKMARK IS ON THIS PAGE, WALLY FOLLOWERS. SO NOW YOU KNOW, THIS IS MY FAVOURITE SCENE! THIS IS THE ONLY SCENE IN THE BOOK WHERE YOU CAN SEE MORE OF THE REAL WOOF THAN JUST HIS TAIL! BUT CAN YOU FIND HIM? HE'S THE ONLY ONE WITH FIVE RED STRIPES ON HIS TAIL! HERE'S ANOTHER CHALLENGE! ELEVEN

TRAVELLERS HAVE FOLLOWED ME HERE – ONE FROM EVERY SCENE. CAN YOU SEE THEM? AND CAN YOU FIND WHERE EACH ONE JOINED ME ON MY ADVENTURES, AND SPOT ALL THEIR APPEARANCES AFTERWARDS? KEEP ON SEARCHING, WALLY FANS! HAVE A WONDERFUL, WONDERFUL TIME!

THE GREAT
WHERE'S WALLY?
THE WONDER BOOK
CHECK LIST

More and more wonderful things
for Wally fans to check out!

ONCE UPON A PAGE...

- Helen of Troy and Paris
- Rudyard Kipling and the jungle book
- Sir Francis and his drake
- Wild Bill hiccup
- A shopping centaur
- Handel's water music
- George washing ton
- Samuel peeps at his diary
- Guy forks
- Tchaikovsky and the nut cracker sweet
- A roundhead with a round head
- Pythagoras and the square of the hippopotamus
- William shakes spear
- Madame two swords
- Garibaldi and his biscuits
- Florence and her nightingale
- The pilgrim fathers
- Captain cook
- Hamlet making an omelette
- Jason and the juggernauts
- Whistling Whistler painting his mother
- Ali barber
- Lincoln and the Gettysburg address
- Stephenson's rocket
- Two knights fighting the war of the roses
- The Duke of Wellington's wellington

THE MIGHTY FRUIT FIGHT

- A box of dates next to a box of dates
- A pair of date palms
- "An apple a day keeps the doctor away"
- Six crab apples
- Four royal oranges
- Blueberries wearing blue berets
- A kiwi fruit
- A banana doing the splits
- A pine apple
- Three fruit fools
- One devil fruit and a can of fruit
- Cranberry sauce
- An orange upsetting the apple cart
- A banana tree
- Cooking apples
- Elder berries wine
- Seven wild cherries
- Goose berries
- A pound of apples
- A partridge on a pear tree
- A fruit cock tail
- Two peach halves
- The Big Apple
- One sour apple without ...
- Paw paw fruit
- Another apple cart be...

THE ODLAW SWAMP

- Two soldiers disguised as Odlaws
- A soldier wearing a bowler hat
- A soldier wearing a stovepipe hat
- A soldier wearing a straw hat
- A soldier wearing a riding helmet
- Three soldiers wearing peaked caps
- A lady wearing an Easter bonnet
- Two soldiers wearing American football helmets
- Two soldiers wearing baseball caps
- A big shield next to a little shield
- A lady wearing a sun hat
- A soldier with two big feathers in his hat
- Some turtle snakes
- Seven wooden rafts
- Five romantic snakes
- Three small wooden boats
- Four birds nests
- One Odlaw in disguise
- A swamp creature without stripes
- A monster cleaning its teeth
- A monster asleep, but not too long
- A soldier floating on a barrel
- A very big monster with a very small head
- One charmed snake
- Five charmed spears
- A snake reading

CLOWN TOWN

- A clown reading a newspaper
- A starry umbrella
- A clown with a blue teapot
- Two hoses leaking
- A clown with two boons on each arm
- A clown looking through a telescope
- Two clowns holding big hammers
- A clown with a bag of crackers
- Two clowns holding flower pots
- A clown swinging a pillow
- A clown combing the roof of a Clown Town house
- A clown bursting a balloon
- Six flowers squirting the same clown
- A clown wearing a jack-in-the-box hat
- Three cars
- A watering-can
- One hat joining two clowns
- A clown with a fishing rod
- A clown about to catapult a custard pie
- Three clowns wearing tea shirts
- A clown with buckets of water
- A clown with a yo-yo
- A clown stepping into a custard pie
- Seventeen clouds
- A clown having his foot tickled
- One clown with a green nose

THE FANTASTIC FLOWER GARDEN

- The yellow rose of Texas
- Flower pots and flower beds
- Butter flies
- Gardeners sowing seeds and planting bulbs
- A garden nursery
- A bird bath and a bird table
- House plants, wall flowers and blue bells
- Dandy lions, tiger lilies and fox gloves
- Cabbage patches, letters leaves and a collie flower
- A hedgehog next to a hedge hog
- A flower border and a flower show
- A bull frog
- Earth worms
- A wheelbarrow full of wheels
- A cricket match
- Parsley, sage, Rosemary and time
- A queen bee near a honey comb
- A landscape gardener
- A sun dial next to a sundial
- Gardeners dancing to the beetles
- A green house and a tree house
- A spring onion and a leek with a leak
- Dor mice
- An apple tree
- Weeping willows and climbing roses
- Rock pool

THE CORRIDORS O...

- Clock striking twelve
- Clock faces
- A cuck hoot
- Wall clock
- A clock tower
- A very loud alarm clock
- A travelling clock
- A runner racing against time
- Roman numerals
- Time flies
- An hour glass
- Big Ben
- Old Father Time
- Grandfather clock
- A walking stick
- Three sets of almost identical twins
- One pair of identical twins
- A man's braces being pulled in opposite directions
- A swinging pendulum
- Coat tails tied in a knot
- A door and thirteen clocks on their sides
- A very tall top hat
- A sundial
- A pair of hooked umbrellas
- A clock cuckoo
- A pair of tangled walking-sticks

THE GAME OF GAMES

- [ ] Some stair cases
- [ ] Maze inside a maze
- [ ] A cross-word
- [ ] A flight of stairs
- [ ] A map reading
- [ ] A player rolling the dice
- [ ] A player walking
- [ ] A player with a map and a pair of compasses
- [ ] One player throwing a six
- [ ] One player not wearing gloves
- [ ] The other lost glove
- [ ] A missing puzzle piece
- [ ] A bad mathematician
- [ ] Eight shovels
- [ ] Twenty-nine hoops
- [ ] Two pots of paint
- [ ] An upside down question-mark on a player's tunic
- [ ] A blue player holding a green block
- [ ] A players with a green block
- [ ] Five referees with their arms folded
- [ ] Five crying players with handkerchiefs
- [ ] Two players reading newspapers
- [ ] A smoke signal
- [ ] Three ticklish players
- [ ] Eight messages in bottles

TOYS! TOYS! TOYS!

- [ ] Two spinning tops and a top spinning
- [ ] Jack in the box
- [ ] A toy soldier being decorated
- [ ] A toy soldier in full dress uniform
- [ ] A toy drill sergeant
- [ ] A fish tank
- [ ] Four baby's bottles
- [ ] Two anchors
- [ ] A toy figure on skis
- [ ] A chalkboard
- [ ] A toy figure pushing a wheelbarrow
- [ ] A crow's-nest
- [ ] An apple tree bookend
- [ ] A goal
- [ ] Five big red books
- [ ] A bear on a rocking-horse
- [ ] A toy bandsman holding cymbals
- [ ] A toy performer balancing two chairs in the air
- [ ] Five wooden soldiers
- [ ] A giraffe with a red-and-white-striped scarf
- [ ] A pirate carrying a barrel
- [ ] Toy figures climbing up a long scarf
- [ ] A teddy bear wearing a green scarf
- [ ] Two giraffes in the ark
- [ ] A robot holding a red tray

BRIGHT LIGHTS AND NIGHT FRIGHTS

- [ ] Street lights
- [ ] Lime light
- [ ] A rowing boat
- [ ] An octo-puss
- [ ] Moon light
- [ ] Light entertainers
- [ ] A very light house
- [ ] Day light
- [ ] A fishing boat
- [ ] A standard lamp
- [ ] Christmas tree lights
- [ ] A light weight boxer
- [ ] Star light
- [ ] A light at the end of the tunnel
- [ ] Stage lights
- [ ] A motor boat
- [ ] A sailor walking the plank
- [ ] A diving board
- [ ] Candle light
- [ ] A bedside light
- [ ] The deep blue C
- [ ] A Chinese lantern
- [ ] A search light
- [ ] A sleeping monster
- [ ] A mirror
- [ ] Four sailors looking through telescopes

THE BATTLE OF THE BANDS

- [ ] A rubber band
- [ ] A piano forte
- [ ] A pipe band
- [ ] Bandsmen "playing" their instruments
- [ ] A fan fair
- [ ] Bandsmen with saxophones and sacks of phones
- [ ] A steel band
- [ ] A swing band
- [ ] Sheet music
- [ ] Racing bandsmen "beating" their drums
- [ ] A rock band
- [ ] Kettle drums
- [ ] A mouth organ
- [ ] A baby sitar
- [ ] A C-man band
- [ ] A French horn
- [ ] A barrel organ
- [ ] Some violin bows
- [ ] A rock and roll band
- [ ] Bandsmen playing cornets
- [ ] A drummer with drum sticks
- [ ] A big elephant trunk
- [ ] Bandsmen making a drum kit
- [ ] An orchestra pit
- [ ] Sand paper
- [ ] Two cheetah bandsmen cheating

THE CAKE FACTORY

- [ ] A loading bay
- [ ] Conveyor belts
- [ ] Two Danish pastries
- [ ] A gingerbread man
- [ ] Two workers blowing cream horns
- [ ] Maple syrup
- [ ] Hot cross buns
- [ ] A Swiss roll
- [ ] A pan cake
- [ ] A chocolate moose
- [ ] A custard pie fight
- [ ] Apple pie
- [ ] Black forest gateau
- [ ] A fish cake
- [ ] Rock cakes
- [ ] Dough nuts
- [ ] A doe nut
- [ ] Baked Alaska pudding
- [ ] A fairy cake
- [ ] Mississippi mud pie
- [ ] Upside down cake
- [ ] Carrot cake
- [ ] A cup cake
- [ ] Sponge cakes
- [ ] A cake carrying a worker

THE LAND OF WOOFS

- [ ] Dog biscuits
- [ ] A mountain dog
- [ ] A hot dog getting cool
- [ ] A grey hound bus
- [ ] Dog baskets
- [ ] A pair of swimming trunks
- [ ] A watch dog
- [ ] A bull dog
- [ ] A great Dane
- [ ] A guard dog
- [ ] A dog in a wet suit
- [ ] Some swimming costumes
- [ ] A dog with a red collar
- [ ] A dog wearing a yellow collar with a blue disc
- [ ] A top dog
- [ ] A sausage dog with sausages
- [ ] A dog wearing a blue collar with a green disc
- [ ] A cat dressed like a Woof dog
- [ ] The puppies' pool
- [ ] A woof doing a paw stand
- [ ] A Scottie dog
- [ ] Two dogs having a massage
- [ ] A sniffer dog
- [ ] Twenty-two red-and-white striped towels

★★★★★ SEEING STARS! ★★★★★

Now it's the end, it's time to go back to the beginning! Remember the first two pages of the book with all the pretty coloured stars on them? Can you spot ten differences between the pictures in the shapes on the left and the pictures in the shapes on the right? And can you find one star shape and one circle shape that both appear four times?

CLOWNING ABOUT!

Ha, ha! What a joker! The clown who follows Wally and his friends has changed the colour of his hat band in one scene! Can you find which scene it is! What colour does his hat band change to?

WHERE'S WALLY?

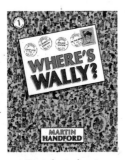

Down the road, over
the sea, around the globe…
Where's Wally? on his
worldwide adventures! Terrific!

Over thousands of years,
past thousands of people…
Where's Wally? now!
Amazing!

Once upon a mermaid,
once upon a dragon…
Where's Wally? in the
realms of fantasy! Magic!

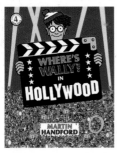

Lights, camera, action…
Where's Wally? behind the
scenes! Cool!

Stepping off the pages, and
into life… Where's Wally?
in lands full of wonder! Wow!

Spot the difference, match the
silhouettes… Where's Wally?
at the gallery! Brilliant!

Have *you* found all six mini books yet?